HARRY TRUMAN

The Presidents of the United States

George Washington
1789–1797

John Adams
1797–1801

Thomas Jefferson
1801–1809

James Madison
1809–1817

James Monroe
1817–1825

John Quincy Adams
1825–1829

Andrew Jackson
1829–1837

Martin Van Buren
1837–1841

William Henry Harrison
1841

John Tyler
1841–1845

James Polk
1845–1849

Zachary Taylor
1849–1850

Millard Fillmore
1850–1853

Franklin Pierce
1853–1857

James Buchanan
1857–1861

Abraham Lincoln
1861–1865

Andrew Johnson
1865–1869

Ulysses S. Grant
1869–1877

Rutherford B. Hayes
1877–1881

James Garfield
1881

Chester Arthur
1881–1885

Grover Cleveland
1885–1889

Benjamin Harrison
1889–1893

Grover Cleveland
1893–1897

William McKinley
1897–1901

Theodore Roosevelt
1901–1909

William H. Taft
1909–1913

Woodrow Wilson
1913–1921

Warren Harding
1921–1923

Calvin Coolidge
1923–1929

Herbert Hoover
1929–1933

Franklin D. Roosevelt
1933–1945

Harry Truman
1945–1953

Dwight Eisenhower
1953–1961

John F. Kennedy
1961–1963

Lyndon B. Johnson
1963–1969

Richard Nixon
1969–1974

Gerald Ford
1974–1977

Jimmy Carter
1977–1981

Ronald Reagan
1981–1989

George H. W. Bush
1989–1993

William J. Clinton
1993–2001

George W. Bush
2001–2009

Barack Obama
2009–

HARRY TRUMAN

WIL MARA

 **Marshall Cavendish**
Benchmark
New York

Published by Marshall Cavendish Benchmark
An imprint of Marshall Cavendish Corporation

Other Marshall Cavendish Offices:
Marshall Cavendish International (Asia) Private Limited, 1 New Industrial Road, Singapore 536196 • Marshall Cavendish International (Thailand) Co Ltd. 253 Asoke, 12th Flr, Sukhumvit 21 Road, Klongtoey Nua, Wattana, Bangkok 10110, Thailand • Marshall Cavendish (Malaysia) Sdn Bhd, Times Subang, Lot 46, Subang Hi-Tech Industrial Park, Batu Tiga, 40000 Shah Alam, Selangor Darul Ehsan, Malaysia

Marshall Cavendish is a trademark of Times Publishing Limited

All websites were available and accurate when this book was sent to press.

Library of Congress Cataloging-in-Publication Data

Mara, Wil.
Harry Truman / Wil Mara.
p. cm. — (Presidents and their times)
Includes bibliographical references and index.
Summary: "Provides comprehensive information on President Harry Truman and places him within his historical and cultural context. Also explored are the formative events of his times and how he responded"—Provided by publisher.
ISBN 978-1-60870-185-8 (print) ISBN 978-1-60870-727-0 (ebook)
1. Truman, Harry S., 1884–1972—Juvenile literature. 2. Presidents—United States—Biography—Juvenile literature.
3. United States—Politics and government—1945–1953—Juvenile literature. I. Title.
E814.M34 2012
973.918092—dc22 [B] 2010020308

Editor: Christine Florie
Publisher: Michelle Bisson
Art Director: Anahid Hamparian
Series Designer: Alex Ferrari

Photo research by Marybeth Kavanagh

Cover photo by White House, Courtesy of Harry S. Truman Library

The photographs in this book are used by permission and through the courtesy of: *Harry S. Truman Library*, 3, 6, 8, 9, 13, 28, 34, 35, 41, 48, 90, 97, 98L, 99L; *Getty Images*: 78; *Time Life Pictures (Eliot Elisofon)*, 11; *(US Army Signal Corps)*, 23; *(Jerry Cooke/Pix Inc.)*, 52; *(Bernard Hoffman)*, 60; *(John Dominis)*, 83; *Ralph E. Gray/National Geographic*, 93; *Rolls Press/Popperfoto*, 94, 99R; *Alamy: Niday Picture Library*, 15; *Mary Evans Picture Library*, 43; *The Image Works: akg-images*, 19, 37, 98R; *SZ Photo*, 50; *TopFoto*, 68, 72; *SV-Bilderdienst*, 73; *AP Photo*: 24; *Newscom: Harry S. Truman Library and Museum/UPI*, 27; *National Archives/AFP*, 81; *Library of Congress: Harris & Ewing*, 25; *Corbis: Bettmann*, 31, 66; *The Art Archive: Culver Pictures*, 46; *SuperStock*: 58; *Everett Collection*, 54; *Underwood Photo Archives*, 70, 75, 82; *The Granger Collection, NYC*: 63; *Everett Collection: WiscHistorSociety*, 87

Printed in Malaysia
1 3 5 6 4 2

CONTENTS

★ ★ ★ ★ ★ ★ ★ ★ ★ ★ ★ ★ ★ ★ ★ ★ ★

MIDWESTERN BOY

Harry S. Truman was born on May 8, 1884, in Lamar, Missouri. His father, John Anderson Truman, was a farmer who also bought and sold mules and other domesticated animals. He was uneducated but had high ambitions and a willingness to work hard. Harry's mother, Martha Ellen Young Truman (nicknamed Mattie), kept house and watched over Harry and his two younger siblings—a brother, Vivian, and a sister, Mary Jane. Harry was named after his maternal uncle, Harrison Young. He was given the middle initial *S* in honor of both of his grandfathers—Solomon Young and Anderson Shippe Truman—but he did not receive an actual middle name.

After a series of moves during the first several years of his life, Harry and his family settled in the western Missouri town of Independence. Unlike nearby Kansas City, with its rapid growth and urbanized atmosphere, Independence was a quiet and conservative community.

A HAPPY CHILDHOOD

In his later years, Truman said that his childhood had been filled with happiness. He grew up surrounded by members of his extended family—aunts, uncles, grandparents, and cousins—and he loved having them around. He was a cheerful boy, easy to get along with and eager to please. He had an instinct for what made others happy and used it to get approval. He went to fairs, learned

7

Truman adored his mother and had great respect for his father. He would form a strong bond with both of them over time.

card games, played with animals on the farm, and sat out in back of his house to watch trains go by. Railroads were expanding throughout the nation at this time, a period of industrial growth that became known as the Gilded Age. The growth began in the Northeast, where the population was the densest. The era saw the rise of a class of wealthy and prominent businessmen, among them such historic figures as John D. Rockefeller, Andrew Carnegie, and J. P. Morgan. It was only a matter of time before **economic** activity and industrial growth began spreading westward.

Young Harry was likely unaware of these developments as a little boy, as life on the farm kept him busy. He had to do his share of the chores, including feeding the animals and chopping and hauling wood for fires. He always tried his best at whatever he was asked to do, but there was also time to relax and have fun.

Truman's youth was spent surrounded by family. Here he (second on left), family, and friends are photographed on a farm wagon.

As he later remembered, "Vivian and I used to play in the south pasture—a beautiful meadow in bluegrass. At the end of the grove was a mudhole. This grove was row on row of beautiful maple trees, a quarter of a mile long and six rows wide. We had a little red wagon which we took with us on our adventures in the pasture."

Harry developed a strong and lasting bond with both of his parents, although in different ways. Because he was quiet and somewhat shy, his mother was protective of him. Harry was her first child, and she thought the world of him. They remained close until her death in 1947.

Harry's relationship with his father was slower to develop because John Truman worked long hours when Harry was young. John Truman was known for his integrity, which came from a powerful sense of right and wrong. He instilled this morality in Harry from a very young age. While Harry's relationship with his father may not have been as tender as the one he shared with his mother, Harry had great respect for him. Much of his father's character was to serve as a model for the man Harry would eventually become.

Harry spent endless hours reading. After he read the many books in the Truman home, he got a card from the Independence library and began going through its collection. His favorite subject was history, with a particular fondness for military topics. He read about famous wars and legendary figures, and he could quote details of great battles from memory. He also read his family's Bible from cover to cover. One likely reason he preferred reading over the physical activities that boys usually preferred, such as sports, was that he was severely farsighted. He got his first pair of glasses at the age of six and became an inveterate reader.

A Lifelong Love of Music

John Truman served as inspiration for one of Harry's favorite hobbies as a boy—music. As one of Harry's later biographers wrote, "[Harry's father] loved to sing when the family spent time around the piano in the evenings. Harry and his sister, Mary Jane, remembered their father singing hymns in a pleasant, light voice." Harry loved listening to all kinds of music, but he also wanted to play. His family had a piano in the front parlor of their home, at which Harry practiced enthusiastically. He took formal lessons for many years, and soon he was moving past simple standards and playing more difficult classical pieces. He loved music all his life and was known in his adult years as an excellent pianist.

Schooling

Harry was an excellent student. He went about his schoolwork with the same diligence and determination that he applied to his chores at home, and his teachers found him to be bright, curious, and obedient. He almost always earned top grades. He took some tutoring classes the summer following second grade and did so well that he went straight to fourth grade. One of the few times that he got a low grade was in handwriting, and that poor grade has a reasonable explanation—Harry was naturally left-handed, and the school had required him to write with his right hand. In time, however, he mastered writing with his right hand.

Naturally shy as a child, Harry usually kept his distance from girls. At the age of six at the local Presbyterian Sunday school, he saw his future wife for the first time—a little girl with blond hair and blue eyes named Elizabeth Wallace. Although she had made an impression even at that early age, years went by before he worked up the nerve to speak to her. Nicknamed Bessie (which would eventually be shortened to Bess), she lived less than three blocks away from him. In many ways, Bess was Harry's opposite—she was outgoing, popular, fashionable, athletic, and unafraid to speak her mind. She also came from a wealthy family, one of the reasons young Harry—with his working-class roots—was afraid to approach her. Whatever his fears, he overcame them in time and married her.

Harry began high school in the fall of 1897. He still liked history best but now also had an interest in literature. His weakest subjects were science and spelling (he had difficulty with spelling all his life). By his senior year, Harry had become confident

enough in himself to lose some of his shyness, and he begin making new friends. He also began spending time with Bess Wallace. Bess knew the family of Harry's cousins the Nolands, so they saw each other frequently.

A Seed Is Planted

Harry experienced another important development in his life just before the start of his senior year in high school—he had his first taste of the world of politics. In July 1900 he and his father went to the **Democratic National Convention,** in Kansas City. There, the leaders of the Democratic Party nominated William Jennings Bryan—a young lawyer born in Illinois who later settled in Nebraska—as their presidential candidate.

Harry's father's support of Bryan was based on his reputation as a protector of the common man, one who fought the Northeast's wealthy elite and the sometimes corrupt practices through which many lined their own pockets at the expense of ordinary, working Americans. John Truman also liked Bryan's anti-imperialist position following the end of the Spanish-American War. In early 1898 America became involved in a brief military conflict with Spain in response to Spain's oppressive rule of Cuba. Afterward Cuba was given its independence, and America acquired the nations of Guam, Puerto Rico, and the Philippines. In spite of having volunteered for the Spanish-American War, Bryan was firmly against America's control of these nations. He believed it was no more justified than the colonialism that America itself had suffered under Great Britain that led to the Revolutionary War.

Between the huge crowds, the fanfare, and Bryan's inspiring speeches, Harry was dazzled. He later wrote about

A 1900 presidential campaign poster for candidate William Jennings Bryan. The young Harry Truman witnessed his nomination at the Democratic National Convention in Kansas City.

the candidate's legendary speaking ability: "The hall there could hold . . . maybe seventeen thousand people, and I was up on the roof garden. From where I was watching he didn't look more than a foot high, and as I told you he didn't have a microphone, but I could hear every word he said." In spite of Bryan's eventual loss to the Republican candidate, William McKinley, the experience of attending a major political convention left a lasting impression on Harry.

When Harry finished high school in May 1901, he had no specific plans for the future. He considered pursuing a military career and tried to get an appointment to the U.S. Military Academy, at West Point, in New York. If that did not work out, he knew there were always other options.

Two

Rich Man, Poor Man

*T*ruman's hope of attending West Point was dashed owing to his poor eyesight. Other factors kept him from attending college, too. The summer after he graduated from high school, thanks to a severe drop in wheat prices, his father not only lost money through the family farm but also through his investments as a wheat **speculator**. The Truman family was drawn into one of the most difficult financial periods they would ever know. His father was forced to take a job as a night watchman, a job whose salary barely paid the family's bills. As a result, Harry lost any chance of going to college (Truman was the only president in the twentieth century who did not have a college degree).

Working

Truman kept a positive attitude and opted to go to work. This decision led to a series of jobs in the western Missouri area. The first was in Kansas City, in the mailroom of the Kansas City *Star*. Next he worked as a timekeeper for the Santa Fe Railroad, which was being extended through the Kansas City area. During his time on the Santa Fe, Truman was exposed to the kind of men he had seen little of during his childhood—rough and uncultured. They, in turn, were amused by the polite young man from farm country. In spite of the culture shock, however, Truman got along with his coworkers just fine, and they with him.

In the spring of 1903, he left the railroad to take a position as a bank clerk. He did well and impressed his colleagues as well as his bosses. In 1905 he went to another bank largely because the pay was better. To satisfy his ongoing desire for military service, in May 1905 he enlisted in the Missouri National Guard. The National Guard wanted new recruits, and so Truman's poor eyesight was not important. He started as a private but was soon promoted to corporal.

Truman was enjoying city life in Kansas City by this time. He lived in a small apartment, went to local restaurants, and attended the theater. He was also corresponding with Bess. Owing to family circumstances, however, he had to return home in early 1906. John Truman's financial struggles forced him to move to the town of Grandview, about sixteen miles from Independence, and live on the farm belonging to his in-laws, the Youngs. Running the six-hundred-acre farm required more people than the Youngs could afford to hire. So Harry returned to lend a hand.

Though small and slender, Harry put his best effort into farmwork and soon became physically stronger as a result of the hard work. With John Truman's age beginning to slow him down, Harry was given more responsibilities. In time, as the Youngs' land became profitable, Harry was viewed around Grandview as a fine farmer. He used some of the money to help pay down his father's debts.

WORLD WAR I

The price of farm goods rose during the mid–1910s as a result of the outbreak of World War I. The war began in July 1914, after the assassination in June of Archduke Franz Ferdinand of

In 1905 Truman
enlisted in the
Missouri National
Guard.

SELF-DOUBTS

Truman wrote to Bess from Grandview frequently but felt he was getting nowhere with her. After all, she was a young woman from a wealthy family, and he was from a farmer's family. In a letter he received in November 1913, Bess finally made her feelings clear; she said he was the only man she would ever consider marrying. They agreed to become engaged but kept it secret because of Bess's mother, Madge, who would not have approved of Bess's interest in an ordinary farm boy. As one of the schoolteachers from Independence later remembered about Madge Wallace, "Nobody was ever good enough for her, or so it seemed. She was a very, very difficult person. . . . And Harry Truman was not, at that time, a very promising prospect."

Austria-Hungary by a Serbian terrorist. The antagonists consisted of two opposing groups of nations: the **Central Powers** (Austria-Hungary, Germany, and several other nations) and the **Allies** (Great Britain, France, Russia, and Serbia, among others). When the war began, President Woodrow Wilson favored neutrality—as did most other U.S. citizens. American industries, farming among them, would provide supplies, but American forces would not be involved in the fighting.

Truman followed the progress of the war in his spare time, but he had another matter on his mind. The health of John Truman steadily declined throughout 1914 owing to an injury he sustained on the farm early in the year. His refusal to seek immediate medical attention led to complications and an operation in the summer. His health did not improve, however; he died on November 2, 1914. Harry was with him until the end.

In spite of Wilson's promise to keep America out of the war, in his second term, he decided that the Allies needed America's help to gain victory over the Central Powers.

At this time, with America about to enter the war, Truman began to look for another way to make a living. With some of the profits from his work on the farm, he had a little extra money to invest.

He first looked into land speculation, hoping to find some prime real estate at a bargain price. After long and exhausting searches, however, he came up with nothing. He then joined a **consortium** with several other men and put a few thousand dollars into a zinc and lead mine in Oklahoma; that venture failed, and the mine closed in September 1916. Truman then entered a partnership for oil speculation. With America's inevitable involvement in the war, he believed demand would be running high. It was just a matter of finding some good oil deposits. He poured thousands more into this venture, but it also went nowhere.

CAPTAIN HARRY

In early 1917 Germany launched a series of submarine attacks against American vessels. Furthermore, the Germans asked Mexico to launch a ground attack against the United States. Congress responded to this hostility on April 6, 1917, by officially approving U.S. involvement in the war. American troops were sent to Europe a few months later. "Once committed to [the war]," the historian John Keegan wrote, "America's extraordinary capacity for industrial production and human organization took possession of the nation's energies. . . . Over 24 million men

An Opportunity Missed

As if Truman needed more evidence of his bad luck in the business world, it turned out that he gave up on his oil venture too soon. A huge pool was discovered under one of the tracts of land in which he had been interested. This land, located in northeastern Kansas, eventually became known as the Teeter Pool. By the 1940s it was producing more than 15,000 barrels of oil per year. Truman and his partners had miscalculated; they had not drilled deep enough to reach the oil deposits. The strike would have made Truman a millionaire.

were registered in 1917–18 and those deemed most eligible—young and unmarried males without dependents—formed the first contingent of 2,810,000 draftees."

Wanting to contribute to America's role in the war, Truman joined the military in the spring of 1917. He was in his early thirties and still running the Young farm, but his sense of patriotism was strong. He even turned down a suggestion from Bess that they be married. He did not want to turn her into a young widow if he died or burden her with the responsibility of caring for him if he were permanently injured.

The Missouri National Guard made Truman a first lieutenant. He was shipped overseas in March 1918 and in April went to France, where he received combat training and was promoted to captain. By the summer, Truman was ready for action.

In July he was given his first command—the nearly two hundred men of Battery D, better known as Dizzy D. They were a rough bunch who disliked authority and had driven out all of their previous commanders. When they first laid eyes on Truman, they figured he would be an easy target like all the others. "Although they were standing at attention," one later remembered, "you could feel the . . . blood boiling—as much as to say, if this guy thinks he's going to take us over, he's mistaken."

Truman was like no other commander the soldiers of Battery D had faced before. While he was tough on them, he could also be compassionate. He spoke to them as equals, rather than inferiors. He expected them to work hard, but he had the same expectations for himself. Soon the boys of Dizzy D were falling in line behind Truman, whom they nicknamed Captain Harry. Once again his likable nature had worked a miracle—and as a result, his

In 1917 President Woodrow Wilson sent U.S. troops to Europe to help fight the war against the Central Powers.

confidence in himself increased. As Truman's daughter, Margaret, remarked in her writings about her father years later, "He came out of the army convinced that if he could lead these wild men, he could lead anyone."

In March 1918 Germany launched a series of attacks against Allied forces in Belgium and France, hoping to drive them back and capture key territories before U.S. reinforcement troops arrived. The Allies managed to hold their own, however, and by May, American soldiers were arriving on the scene. By the end of the summer, well over a million would be involved.

Truman (third from right behind seated officers) with officers of Dizzy D in France in 1918.

A Missouri Girl at Heart

Elizabeth Virginia "Bess" Wallace was the oldest of four siblings, and, as the other three were all males, she grew up as something of a tomboy. In an age when girls and boys had clearly defined roles and were expected to fulfill them without question, Bess was as unrelenting and athletic as her brothers or any of their friends. It was this toughness that would see her through the many difficult years that lay ahead as a politician's wife. As Truman rose  from one position to another, Bess always did what was expected of her. In truth, however, she did not enjoy her role. She cared little for the pomp and circumstance of official positions, and she possessed no great love of the spotlight. When her husband's political career finally came to an end, she was happy to travel back to Missouri—the only place she ever considered home.

In September 1918 Allied military commanders decided to launch a series of attacks that they hoped would end the war. Truman's Battery D became part of this massive offensive. The fighting, as fierce as any ever recorded, lasted from September to early November. Against all odds, Truman's battery lost only one man; many of the men later said that Truman's leadership was the main reason for their low casualty count.

The Germans, staggered by the massive assault, agreed to a truce on November 11, 1918, thus ending World War I. The following June, Germany was required to sign the Treaty of Versailles. The treaty forced Germany to take blame for causing the war in the first place, compelled it to pay financial reparations for much of the damage done (in the amount of $3 billion, which was a huge sum in 1919), stripped it of land and colonial power over other nations, and plunged it into an economic nightmare.

Truman remained in Europe as part of his military duties until April 1919, at which time he boarded an ocean liner and headed for home. He was formally discharged from the army in May. Not long after returning to Missouri, on June 28, 1919, he and Bess married.

Getting Back to Business

While Truman had been away in Europe, his sister, Mary Jane, ran the Young farm. She had little interest in farming and was more than happy to hand the responsibilities back to her brother upon his return. Truman, however, had other ideas, as did his wife-to-be. "Even before my father came back from France and married Mother," his daughter, Margaret, wrote, "he had made up his mind that he was through with farming. Mother [also]

played a role in this decision. She made it clear that she had no desire to be a farmer's wife."

Truman decided to try his hand at business again. He and an Army friend named Eddie Jacobson had the idea of opening a haberdashery—an outlet for gentlemen's clothing and accessories such as belts, ties, cufflinks, hats, and shirts. Some of the start-up money came from a bank loan, the rest from their personal savings. Truman also raised some cash by selling off equipment and livestock from the farm.

Truman and Jacobson Men's Furnishing, selling only the finest-quality merchandise, opened in Kansas City in November 1919.

Truman and Army friend Eddie Jacobson opened a men's garment shop in Kansas City in 1919.

The American economy was strong at this time, and business boomed. A steady stream of Army buddies became loyal customers. All seemed to be going well. Then, in 1920 the economy began to slide, and business at Truman and Jacobson took a turn for the worse. By 1921 the nation was caught in the grip of a deep recession. Prices began to tumble, and money was suddenly in short supply.

Truman and Jacobson were forced to close the store in 1922. With debts of around $35,000 (of which $12,000 was Truman's), they could have filed for bankruptcy. It would have wiped out the debt but left the store's **creditors** with enormous losses. Truman, believing it was dishonest and unethical, refused to file. He began paying down his share of the debt a little at a time (it took two decades). After this business failure, Truman once again thought about finding a new career.

POLITICS

Three

His business aspirations in ruins and not happy at the prospect of more years toiling on the Young farm, Truman had to consider new options. He was intelligent, well-read, and respected by all who knew him. On the other hand, he had no college education and little experience in other professions. With a new wife and steep debts, he needed a fresh direction.

THE PENDERGAST MACHINE

Truman's salvation came in the form of a man named Tom Pendergast. A resident of Kansas City, Pendergast was the head of the most powerful Democratic **political machine** in the area. He never held political office; he preferred to control the political process from behind the scenes. His way of running things was not always honest, however. Police were often given bribes to look the other way when Pendergast broke the law. Journalists were paid to write flattering stories and to ignore those that might put Pendergast in a bad light. People who turned against him were intimidated, threatened, or even beaten. On election day, ballot boxes were stuffed with fake votes to make sure Pendergast-supported candidates won their races.

There was another side to Tom Pendergast, however. He looked out for the interests of the poor people. He made sure jobs were available to anyone who needed one and that people who had fallen on hard times received necessities such as food and clothing. Anyone in need of a loan or a place to sleep could go to Pendergast for help. So in spite of his corrupt political practices,

Tom Pendergast was the head of one of the most powerful political machines in Kansas City history. He took a liking to Harry Truman, and through Pendergast, Truman was able to launch his political career.

he was looked upon by many in the Kansas City area as a kind of folk hero. "I'm kind to people," he once said to a biographer. "I like to be kind to people. I never give an argument when a man comes in for a dollar or wants help. . . . Maybe he wants a job. I always go out of my way to help."

Truman came to know Tom Pendergast through Tom's nephew, Jim. Jim and Harry had been friends for many years. Jim admired Truman's sense of honesty and decency. He also admired the bravery Truman had shown in combat during the war. Jim and Tom wanted to make Truman the "eastern judge" in the three-person Jackson County court (the "western judge" and a presiding judge were the two other positions). Unlike a typical judgeship, this was an administrative position, one that had nothing to do with the courts. These Missouri judges had the power to make decisions concerning the spending of tax dollars, which included hiring people for county jobs, awarding construction contracts, and making civic improvements.

Truman's reputation and his appeal to others who lived in the farmland regions of Jackson County were in his favor. Some thought the straitlaced Truman and the machine boss Tom Pendergast would be a strange combination. One of Truman's biographers later wrote, "They were fundamentally opposites. Truman was a country man, Pendergast a city man. Truman was sometimes emotional, Pendergast never so. . . . But there were attractions to [Truman], and they caught Pendergast's attention. They fitted the boss's needs exactly."

For Truman, the election was a chance to further his interest in politics, as well as provide a much-needed change of profession. He won fairly easily because, quite simply, "Boss Tom" Pendergast wanted him to win it. It was his first political victory.

Judge Truman

Truman decided from the start that he would make his mark as a civic administrator with honesty and efficiency. One of the promises he had made to the voters was improvement of the local roadways. As soon as he got into office, he went about familiarizing himself with all the roads and bridges, and he drove through the county to see their condition for himself. Many of them were in a shocking and sometimes dangerous state of disrepair owing to dishonest managers who had been running the maintenance crews, and overblown contracts that put money in the pockets of people who did very little work in return. Truman led a crusade to weed out these corrupt individuals, award contracts to more-deserving construction companies, and get the roads and bridges back into good shape.

He also discovered a huge amount of debt in the county budget. By reviewing the county's expenses line by line, he was able to cut out wasteful spending and slash the debt in half. To further familiarize himself with the legalities of his job, Truman enrolled in the Kansas City School of Law in his spare time (he attended for two years but did not earn a degree). Even critics of the Pendergast machine were impressed with Truman.

Another important turning point in Truman's life occurred around this time—he became a father. On February 17, 1924, Bess gave birth to a girl. The Trumans named her Mary Margaret in honor of her aunt Mary Jane and her grandmother Margaret Gates Wallace. Truman doted on her from the start.

At the end of his first term as a county judge, which lasted two years, Truman suffered his first political defeat—he failed to get reelected. It was something of a shock to all who knew him, particularly considering the superb job he had done. Even the Kansas City *Star*, which had been critical of the Pendergast machine many times in the past, commented favorably before the election: "The record of the county court is refreshing. . . . Expenditures of the court last year were more than $640,000 less than those of the previous year. To date the deficit has been reduced nearly one half, and there is now a cash balance of more than a million dollars." A writer in the *Sentinel* said, "To even talk about throwing [Truman] out of office after two years of faithful service would be to destroy the incentive for a public official to make good." Nevertheless, Truman lost to his Republican opponent.

Truman believed he could win reelection in two years if he chose to run again. In the meantime, he needed something to do. He got a job selling memberships to

On February 17, 1924, the Trumans welcomed a daughter, Mary Margaret.

the Automobile Club of Kansas City. He also continued with his duties in the Missouri army reserve, and he was an active member of the **Freemasons**.

In the fall of 1926, Truman returned to politics just as he had planned—by winning reelection to the Jackson County court. This time around he ran as the head judge of the three-judge panel, a position that carried a four-year term. He served two terms (he was reelected in 1930). Newspapers noted that they could find no evidence of any type of corruption in the way Truman ran the county's business, in spite of his connection to the Pendergasts. During his eight years Truman succeeded in keeping his earlier promise to make Jackson County's roads the best in the state; he did so by giving contracts only to construction firms with solid reputations. Truman could not stand the "favors system," which awarded contracts to well-connected people who did not deserve them. "The county was in debt when I got in

Truman (second from right) is sworn in for his second term as judge of Jackson County on January 6, 1931.

because the previous occupants of the job were the kind who were always standing with their hands out when contracts were let for buildings or roads or anything at all," Truman said later. "I put a stop to it."

The Great Depression

When the New York Stock Exchange collapsed in October 1929, there began a period of unprecedented economic collapse, the Great Depression. The seeds of the Depression had been planted following World War I, when most of Europe was struggling to get through the aftereffects of the conflict. The war itself had been costly enough, but when it ended, Europe faced the cost of rebuilding its battle-scarred lands. Thus, Europe's economies were in shambles.

Harry the Builder

Among his many achievements as Jackson County's presiding judge, Truman arranged to build a new county hospital and a new courthouse in Kansas City and to complete remodeling of the old courthouse in Independence. These were very ambitious projects, the likes of which had rarely been seen in Jackson County. Truman had the full support of the Pendergasts, most of the media, and the voters. When Tom Pendergast pushed Truman to give contracts to various Pendergast "friends," Truman refused. While Truman's response may have angered Tom, it also gave the Pendergast machine a touch of honesty and credibility it had otherwise been lacking.

Unemployed men search for work on the streets of Chicago during the Great Depression.

In America, the 1920s had been a "boom" decade in many ways. There was increased demand for new products such as cars, radios, and kitchen appliances. There was also a new way to acquire these things—on credit. Credit was a "get it now, pay for it later" plan. Many people spent more than they could afford to pay back. By the end of the 1920s, the nation's financial system was nearing a breaking point. That point was reached on Thursday, October 24, 1929—a date known as Black Thursday—and hit a climax on Tuesday, October 29, 1929. Investors across the nation lost millions of dollars, and banks and other businesses went under. By the winter of 1933, one out of every four people did not have a job. Since America's economy was closely tied to the economies of other major nations, the rest of the world suffered as well.

The farming industry was one of the hardest hit. Truman tried to do what he could for the citizens in Jackson County who were suffering. He received pleas for jobs almost every day. Men who had educations and college degrees could not even earn money doing menial tasks. Some were willing to work just for food. There simply were not enough jobs to go around.

From Missouri to Washington

As the dark days of the 1930s progressed, Truman once again found himself facing a difficult decision. He knew he had done good work as a Jackson County judge, but when his second term was over in January 1935, he was ready for a new challenge. He decided he wanted to make a run for Missouri's governorship. He was well known and well respected, and he had many friends who would support him. He knew, however, that the most important support would have to come from Tom Pendergast.

When he learned that Pendergast was already supporting a different candidate, Truman then suggested that he be allowed to run for a seat in the House of Representatives. Pendergast suggested the Senate instead, and Truman agreed. "[Truman] was coming to the end of his second, and by custom last, term as presiding judge," wrote one biographer, "and he had no other political possibility in mind. . . . He accepted at once."

The first step for Truman was earning the nomination from Missouri's Democratic Party. There were two other Missouri politicians who also wanted it, both of whom were more experienced than Truman. His opponents knew that Truman's greatest strength was his support from the Pendergast machine—but they also knew that that connection could be used against him. They reminded voters of Pendergast's corrupt practices, the implication being that Truman was nothing more than a Pendergast puppet and therefore must also be corrupt. Truman chose not to use these mudslinging tactics against his opponents; he talked instead about the issues that were most important to voters—specifically, the ongoing effects of the Great Depression and what he planned to do about them. In the end, Truman's issue-based approach won him the nomination by more than 40,000 votes.

He had a much easier time in the general election. His opponent was the **incumbent** senator Roscoe C. Patterson. Patterson's greatest obstacle to winning reelection was not Truman but rather the fact that he was a Republican. Because the Great Depression had started during the presidency of the Republican Herbert Hoover, Republicans had had considerable difficulty holding on to political power in many parts of the nation. When Franklin D. Roosevelt, a Democrat, succeeded Hoover in the White House in early 1933, he proposed a group of government programs whose aim was summarized as the three *R*s: relief, reform, and recovery. The fact that many in the nation supported Roosevelt's efforts, which were called the New Deal, made it easier for other Democratic candidates to win elections. Riding the wave of New Deal enthusiasm, Truman defeated Patterson by a wide margin on November 6, 1934.

A Rough Start

Truman's senatorial career got off to a somewhat rough start. He did not arrive in Washington brimming with confidence. He remembered Pendergast's advice—"Work hard, keep your mouth shut, and answer your mail." In essence, Pendergast was telling him to be humble and learn everything that he could (and not to forget who helped him get there). To get ahead, Truman knew

he would have to make friends with Senate veterans who could show him the ropes.

Making friends in the Senate did not prove easy. In spite of Truman's personal honesty and integrity, he was not taken seriously. Although a few senators greeted Truman warmly from the start and offered their advice and assistance, others regarded him as illegitimate owing to his ties to the Pendergast machine—in their eyes, a collection of thugs, thieves, and criminals. A few even refused to speak to him. As one writer remembered, "In the Senate he was . . . ignored. He received a desk in the last row on the Democratic side. In the office building his suite consisted of three rooms on the second floor looking out on the grass-covered inner court. Only a few senators showed any consideration."

In spite of his troubles, Truman poured his energies into learning all that he could by keeping his mouth shut and his eyes and ears open. The tactic backfired, however. Because of his unwillingness to take a stand on any major issue in the Senate, he came to be called "Go-Along, Get-Along Harry" and was regarded as a man of little importance. When Truman introduced a piece of legislation of his own (to provide insurance on farm mortgages), the proposal went nowhere. Another blow came when Bess decided to return to Independence with their daughter, Margaret. Although Truman did not try to stop her, he was soon missing her and wrote to her constantly.

Turning Things Around

Truman's response to these difficulties was to work harder than ever and become the best senator he could. He arrived at his office in the Capitol at seven o'clock each morning and usually returned home for dinner at seven in the evening. Even after he

A Presidential Snub

Even President Roosevelt, whose New Deal programs Truman had supported, gave the new senator the cold shoulder. When Truman first arrived in Washington, he had to wait several months before meeting Roosevelt (it was customary for a new senator to meet the president much sooner). Furthermore, when Truman finally did get an audience with the president, he was given only seven minutes rather than the customary fifteen. If Truman tried to contact Roosevelt on an official matter, his call often went  unreturned. On the rare occasion that he did get a response, it was from an aide and never from the president himself. It became no secret around Washington that Roosevelt considered Truman and his Pendergast connection an embarrassment to the Democratic Party.

got home, he continued poring over books and papers so that he could be knowledgeable on all the issues. Eventually he was assigned to two important committees: the Appropriations Committee and the Interstate Commerce Commission. The former was responsible in part for how government money would be spent. The latter was concerned with the nation's transportation system, a subject about which Truman had some expertise from his Jackson County days.

While in the Senate, Truman also established himself as a man willing to fight corruption in big business. He and another senator, the Montana Democrat Burton Wheeler, investigated the reorganization of the nation's largest railroad system. The government invested millions of dollars during the 1920s and the late 1930s to improve and expand the railroad. However, much of the money ended up in the pockets of dishonest lawyers, railroad executives, and other businessmen.

Truman launched an all-out investigation, and he did not let up even when he found evidence of corruption among railroad officials in his home state of Missouri. He brought in dozens of witnesses during the succession of hearings that uncovered the details of their scheme. He and Senator Wheeler also got President Roosevelt to sign into law the Transportation Act of 1940, which increased government **regulation** of the railroad business.

A New Threat

As the 1930s progressed, President Roosevelt found himself increasingly troubled by more than just corrupt business practices at home. In Europe, problems caused by the aftereffects of both World War I and the Great Depression were beginning to grow. For example, the Treaty of Versailles had left Germany with huge debts, uncontrollable **inflation**, a crippled military, depleted resources, and global humiliation. Frustrated by their government's inability to improve the situation, the German people elected Adolf Hitler as their leader. At one time penniless, Hitler had become the head of the Nazi Party and used the desperation of the German people to elevate himself to power. In 1933, after he had become the nation's chancellor, he outlawed all other political parties. He also defied the Treaty of Versailles by rebuilding Germany's military.

Around the same time, Japan began a campaign to enhance its position in eastern Asia. Japan had fought as one of the Allies in World War I and, as a result, had gained prestige, resources, and political influence. The Japanese were interested in getting more, however. They had already invaded nearby Manchuria (most of which lies within northeastern China) in 1931, with the intent of ultimately conquering China in its entirety.

Hitler invaded Poland in alliance with the Soviet Union in September 1939. He soon after invaded Denmark, Norway, Belgium, Luxembourg, Holland, and France.

President Roosevelt began selling war matériel to Allied nations shortly after Hitler invaded Poland, but he wanted to keep America out of the actual fighting. Truman supported the president but knew, as in the case of World War I, it was unlikely they would be able to remain neutral for very long.

REELECTION

Truman's senatorial career nearly ended after just one term. In the late 1930s an investigation had been launched into the political and business dealings of Tom Pendergast. Federal officials found evidence of everything from bribery and voter fraud to tax

Newspaper headlines at a New York newsstand announce the 1939 invasion of Poland.

evasion, and Pendergast was sentenced in 1939 to more than a year in prison. When Truman launched his reelection campaign in early 1940, two other Missouri Democrats who wanted his Senate seat used the Pendergast story against him in an attempt to beat him out of the Democratic nomination. A further blow came when President Roosevelt refused to support Truman.

So Truman had to go it alone. With the energy and optimism for which he became famous, he gave dozens of speeches and interviews. During his campaigning, he refused to deny his association with Tom Pendergast, a show of loyalty that impressed many voters. As for the Pendergast investigation, when it was completed and Pendergast sent to prison, the courts had found no evidence that Truman himself had committed any wrongdoings. In the end, Truman was renominated by his party, and in 1940 he won the general election against his Republican opponent, Manvel Davis, by more than 40,000 votes. He won an election this time without help from Pendergast; he was coming back to Washington as his own man. When he returned to the Senate, many of his fellow senators had a new respect for him.

THE TRUMAN COMMITTEE

Not long after he began his second senatorial term, Truman found himself once again fighting corruption in business. With the nation gearing up for a role in World War II, billions of government dollars were being poured into lucrative contracts for everything from the manufacture of uniforms and ammunition to the purchase of land for training camps. It was not long before Truman began receiving letters from angry constituents concerning how much money was being wasted owing to gross mismanagement and poor organization.

Rather than rely on secondhand reports of the problem, Truman drove thousands of miles around the country to see for himself. What he found shocked him—expensive material lying unprotected in the rain and snow getting ruined, hundreds of workers doing nothing all day, contractors sending the government padded bills in order to increase their profits, and the best contracts being given out to a favored few businesses rather than through fair competition. When he returned to Washington in February 1941, he asked both President Roosevelt and the Senate to form a committee with himself as chairman to look into the matter. It was called the Senate Special Committee to Investigate the National Defense Program but became known as the Truman Committee.

The "Truman Committee," as it became known, was formed to investigate corrupt business practices concerning government contracts as the nation readied itself for World War II.

As with the investigation into the railroad affair, Truman went into this one with dedication. He spent hundreds of hours learning exactly how the government's defense spending worked and then brought in witness after witness for interviews. When the hearings finally came to an end and all practices of wasteful spending were uncovered, Truman succeeded in saving the government—and, in turn, the American taxpayers—around $15 billion.

The War and the White House

By late 1941 Japan had begun to view the United States as an enemy in spite of the fact that it had not yet engaged in combat. When the Japanese decided to invade Thailand and the Philippines, they included in their plans a strike against the U.S. naval forces stationed at Pearl Harbor, on the Hawaiian island of Oahu. On December 7, more than 350 Japanese planes carried out a surprise bombing campaign on the Pearl Harbor base. More than 2,300 U.S. soldiers and citizens were killed, four battleships were sunk, and other military ships were heavily damaged. Congress declared war on Japan the next day.

Even after America's involvement in the war, Hitler's armies made progress throughout 1942. By September they were moving into every sector of Europe, but then a number of military failures marked the beginning of change. Hitler tried unsuccessfully to conquer Great Britain through a series of air strikes. He also tried to move his forces deep into Russian territory, but the brutal Russian winter stopped them in their tracks. The Allied powers then launched a series of their own attacks beginning in 1943. They invaded Sicily in July 1943 and crossed into mainland Italy in September. In June 1944 they landed in Normandy,

Headlines from the December 9, 1941, New York Times *announcing the declaration of war after the bombing of Pearl Harbor.*

France, and succeeded in ridding Europe of most Nazi occupation by the end of the year. These were enormous blows for Hitler.

With Truman continuing his oversight of defense spending throughout the war, his reputation as an honest and efficient public servant spread. As the Democratic National Convention approached in the summer of 1944, rumors that he was being considered as a possible vice presidential candidate began. There was little doubt that Roosevelt would be renominated by the Democratic Party for a fourth term, but many believed he needed a new running mate. His current vice president, Henry Wallace, was considered by Republicans (as well as more than a few conservative Democrats) to be too **liberal** in his political beliefs. Wallace believed in government control over big business, increased power for labor unions, and civil rights issues, and he occasionally opposed the administration on key foreign policy matters. Another important factor was Roosevelt's health, which was beginning to diminish owing to the strain of his long service in the presidency. Pulling the United States out of the Great Depression and managing the nation's involvement in World War II had changed his appearance; Roosevelt had become frail and gaunt. He also suffered from heart disease. Many doubted he would even survive a fourth term; if he died in office, his vice president would take over as president. Thus the choice of a vice presidential candidate was an important one.

At the start of the convention, which began in July in Chicago, there were two leading candidates for the vice presidency: incumbent vice president Henry Wallace and James Byrnes, a former Supreme Court justice and South Carolina senator. Wallace offended conservative Democrats. Byrnes, on the other hand, offended liberals; his support of **segregationist** policies, for example, could not be ignored by those who believed in equal treatment of all minorities. It soon became clear to those in attendance that the Democratic Party would have to find a candidate who would please both sides. It had to be someone liked and respected who did not have political enemies, held moderate views, and would be able to take over the presidency if necessary. Eventually the delegates settled on Harry Truman.

Owing to Roosevelt's poor health, as well as the ongoing demands of World War II on the president, Truman had to do a

Senator Harry Truman campaigns as vice presidential candidate for Franklin Delano Roosevelt in late 1943.

great deal of campaigning on the president's behalf that autumn. He pushed himself as hard as ever. Roosevelt's Republican opponent, Thomas E. Dewey, the governor of New York, tried to bring up Truman's Pendergast association again, as well as his many business failings. In the end, however, none of the mudslinging worked. On November 8, 1944, the Roosevelt-Truman ticket easily beat the Dewey-Bricker ticket with 432 **electoral votes** to the latter's 99. The popular-vote margin was more than three million.

"Pray for Me Now"

In early February 1945, President Roosevelt—who was not keeping Truman updated on the latest developments in the war—went to a secret meeting with the leaders of Great Britain and the Soviet Union, Winston Churchill and Joseph Stalin respectively, to discuss the reorganization of Europe following the end of the war. This meeting was held in the Soviet Crimean resort of Yalta and was thus known as the Yalta Conference.

Meanwhile, Truman settled into his role as vice president. He presided over the Senate, a task that was one of the vice president's duties, and attended official and social functions. One of his accomplishments during this period was to help confirm

A Reluctant Candidate

For a time, Truman was not sure he even wanted the vice presidential nomination. He had reached a point in his senatorial career where he was very content. He had learned how to get things done in the Senate, and he had built a good name for himself. He was popular with most of his constituents back home, and he had overcome the stigma of being associated with the Pendergast machine. On the other hand, there was a part of him that relished the idea of a new position and new challenges—and the distinct possibility of stepping into the presidency itself. He also believed he had a responsibility to the Democratic Party to bridge the gap between the liberal and conservative factions while maintaining party unity. In the end, he accepted the nomination.

Roosevelt's new secretary of commerce—the president's former vice president Henry Wallace. Wallace had taken the loss to Truman in good spirits and immediately supported the Roosevelt-Truman campaign.

Shortly after Truman was sworn in on January 26, 1945, Tom Pendergast died. In spite of being warned against it, Truman attended the funeral; he was the only public official to do so. Truman felt it was the right thing to do.

Chief Justice Harlan Stone swears in Harry Truman as president of the United States on April 12, 1945.

By all accounts, Truman enjoyed the vice presidency very much. Those who knew him well were pleased to see that, in spite of his new position and power, he still displayed his usual humble, midwestern charm.

Truman's service as vice president was short. On April 12, just eighty-two days after he had taken office, he received a phone call shortly after 5:00 p.m. summoning him to the White House. When he arrived, he was taken to Roosevelt's private quarters on the second floor, where the first lady, Eleanor Roosevelt, told him that the president was dead. When Truman asked the first lady if there was anything he could do for her, she replied, "Is there anything *we* can do for *you*? For you are the one in trouble now."

World War II was not yet over, and Truman knew very little about what Roosevelt had been doing. Nevertheless, the job was now his and his alone. He was sworn in as the thirty-third president of the United States shortly after 7:00 p.m. that evening. One of his first comments to the awaiting press corps was, "Boys, if you ever pray, pray for me now."

Five

FIRST TERM AS PRESIDENT

The most pressing matter Truman had to deal with when he took over the presidency was bringing the war to an end. In the European **theater**, Hitler's forces had been driven from virtually all major towns and cities, their supplies were exhausted, and they had endured heavy casualties. Nevertheless Hitler, hiding in a bunker in the German capital of Berlin, was telling his people to continue the fight. "The situation for Germany was quite hopeless," wrote one World War II historian. "Hitler, however, was not tempted to surrender. Instead, he ordered his soldiers to defend the capital 'to the last man and the last shot,' and he mustered up a home guard . . . made up of ill-equipped overage men and underage boys."

In the Pacific theater, Japanese forces were also reeling. The previous February, U.S. troops attacked them in Manila, recaptured territories in the Philippines, and invaded the island of Iwo Jima. In March, American B-29 bombers pounded Tokyo, Japan's capital city, and mined Japanese harbors to disrupt the nation's shipping. By the beginning of April, U.S. ground troops had begun the invasion of Japan's Ryukyu Islands—specifically, Okinawa. In spite of very heavy losses, the Japanese refused the Allied demand for unconditional surrender. "For the Japanese warrior, the only honorable alternative to victory was death," said one World War II author. "The militarist government of

Japan had done its utmost to [teach] the ordinary civilian this same ethic of death before the dishonor of surrender."

Just weeks after Truman took office, the end of the fighting in Europe was in sight. With the war hopelessly lost and Russian tanks rolling through the streets of Berlin, Hitler committed suicide in his bunker on April 30, 1945. One week later, on May 7, the new German president, Karl Dönitz, authorized the surrender to Allied forces in France. The next day, another German declaration of surrender was given to Soviet forces in Berlin. May 8 was then declared VE (Victory in Europe) Day, and millions around the world celebrated. Truman had mixed feelings about the occasion—he was pleased that fighting in Europe had finally come to an end, but he was deeply concerned that the Japanese still showed no intention of giving up. Although Japanese forces continued to lose ground, their leadership announced in early June that they would fight to the last man.

In mid–July, Truman met with Winston Churchill and Joseph Stalin in the German town of Potsdam, for what became known as the Potsdam Conference. The three leaders discussed Germany's role in postwar Europe, as well as what to do about the ongoing conflict with the Japanese. Out of this meeting came the Potsdam Declaration, which called for Japan's immediate surrender.

When Japanese leaders still refused to surrender, Truman found himself in a very difficult position. During one of his first briefings as president, he was told of a new weapon the United States had secretly developed that possessed awesome force: the atomic bomb. Now Truman had to consider the cost of using the bomb to force Japan's surrender. The destruction that

Winston Churchill, Harry Truman, and Joseph Stalin (left to right) at the Potsdam Conference in July 1945.

would result was almost too horrible to comprehend. Dropping an atomic bomb on a major Japanese city would kill tens of thousands of people in a matter of seconds, and thousands more would be sentenced to slow agonizing deaths from radiation sickness. In addition, the majority of the victims would not be soldiers but rather ordinary citizens, including women and children.

Truman did not want to use the bomb, but his military commanders assured him that the other option—to continue fighting a conventional war—would likely cause hundreds of thousands of deaths on both sides and drag the war on for months, perhaps even years. So at the end of July, Truman approved the use of the cataclysmic weapon. On August 6, the first atomic bomb, nicknamed Little Boy, was dropped over the Japanese city of Hiroshima. It killed about 75,000 people upon detonation and injured nearly that many more. When Japanese leaders still did not surrender, on August 9 Truman ordered the use of a second bomb; known as Fat Man, it was dropped on the city of Nagasaki. The total number of immediate deaths there has never been determined but is believed to be somewhere around 60,000.

The American military, with Truman's approval, planned to drop more atomic bombs in the coming weeks if necessary. However, Japan finally offered an unconditional surrender on August 14, and World War II was over. Truman would later write privately, "In 1945 I had the A Bomb dropped on Japan at two

On August 6, 1945, the first atomic bomb was dropped on the Japanese city of Hiroshima by U.S. forces, leading the way to Japanese surrender.

places. . . . We were at war. We were trying to end it in order to save the lives of our soldiers and sailors. The new bomb was a powerful new weapon of war. In my opinion it had to be used to end the unnecessary slaughter on both sides."

KEEPING THE PEACE

After World War II, Truman and other world leaders focused their energies on the reorganization and rebuilding of Europe and Asia. They also wanted to make sure the peace for which so many had died was maintained.

One of the greatest threats to these goals was the tension that had begun to grow between the United States and the Soviet Union—a tension that would become known as the cold war. Although the two superpowers had fought together as allies, they now began to disagree about the future of Europe and Asia. The Soviets had occupied much of eastern Europe during the war, and now they wanted to hold on to those territories and rule them through their **communist** government. The United States and other nations wanted the war-torn nations of Europe to become free and **democratic**. Nevertheless, Stalin's forces gradually took control of Finland, Bulgaria, Czechoslovakia, Poland, Lithuania, Latvia, Estonia, and Romania. Germany, which was still occupied by Soviet and U.S. military forces, was split in two—West Germany and East Germany, with the United States governing the former and the Soviets the latter.

The tension between the United States and the Soviets grew. Truman became convinced that communism had to be stopped from spreading—a strategy known as containment. In March 1947, he announced to Congress a new foreign policy, which became known as the Truman Doctrine. It stated that America, as the champion of freedom and democracy in the world, was willing to support any nation, militarily or otherwise, that had fallen under the threat of communist rule. Through the Truman Doctrine, the United States sent aid to Greece and Turkey that same year. Truman feared Stalin might try to occupy both countries as they struggled in the war's aftermath.

The Marshall Plan, which was launched in June 1947, was another effort by the Truman administration to stop the spread of communism. It dedicated billions of dollars to restarting the economies of select European nations. The funding was not aimed so much at rebuilding after the war but rather at improving and modernizing major industries and other businesses (in addition, some money was used for the purchase of basic necessities). The hope was that a nation able to stand on its own would be better able to resist pressure from the Soviet Union. The actual name of the plan was the European Recovery Program, but it took on its popular name because of its guidance and support by then-Secretary of State George C. Marshall.

Troubles at Home

Less than a month after the end of World War II, Truman found himself engulfed in numerous domestic difficulties. The American people were eager to return to some sense of normalcy. Everyone, it seemed, wanted or needed something—a good job, a new home, an increase in wages.

What's in a Name?

It was no coincidence that Truman's programs were called the Fair Deal, a name similar to Franklin D. Roosevelt's New Deal. Many Republicans, as well as a fair share of conservative Democrats, had been opposed to various parts of Roosevelt's New Deal, but they went along because the nation was in dire straits at the time, first with the Great Depression and then with World War II. Now Truman faced a Congress that was not willing to be quite so supportive. After many years of New Deal policies, the American people were ready to see the government play a smaller role in their lives, not a larger one.

A political cartoon from 1947 titled "The Way Back" comments on the Marshall Plan, officially known as the European recovery program, proposed by U.S. Secretary of State George C. Marshall.

In September 1945 Truman presented Congress with a highly ambitious domestic program to address some of these problems. Containing twenty-one main points, the proposal covered many issues, including tax reforms, an increase in the nation's minimum wage, federal assistance to those looking to buy homes, national health insurance, and more opportunities for minorities. It was the start of what would become known as the Fair Deal program. It was also the true start, in Truman's mind, of his presidency, as opposed to the continuation of Roosevelt's. "This twenty-one-point message," he later wrote, "marked the beginning of the 'Fair Deal,' and September 6, 1945, is the date that symbolizes for me my assumption of the office of President in my own right."

Because of stiff resistance in Congress, many but not all of Truman's Fair Deal proposals went nowhere. The Housing Act was passed in 1949 during his second term. It provided increased mortgage insurance, financing for low-income citizens in rural communities, and more financing for urban renewal projects. Concerning civil rights, the Fair Deal helped to eradicate racist policies in the American military; it also denied lucrative business opportunities to companies that had a record of racist practices. Another second-term victory was the Social Security Act Amendments of 1950, which extended Social Security benefits for millions of elderly citizens. Although Truman was disappointed by the lack of progress on national health care, the administration's effort served as a driving force behind the creation of **Medicare** during the presidency of Lyndon B. Johnson in the mid–1960s. Truman and his wife were present when Johnson signed Medicare into law in July 1965, and Johnson gave Truman the very first Medicare membership card ever issued.

LABOR VERSUS MANAGEMENT

Almost immediately following World War II, tensions in America between labor and management began to rise. Generally speaking, labor, which represented the average workingman, was interested in pay increases for workers and some kind of government control over the prices of goods and services. On the other side was management, which represented business leaders and other executives, who were interested in just the opposite—they wanted to keep workers' salaries low and stood firmly against the idea of the government interfering in how much they could charge for their products. Both sides worked together to support the nation's effort during World War II. Now that the war was over, the quarreling began anew.

When labor unions in various industries demanded pay hikes to make up for lost wages during the war and to combat rising inflation, employers refused. In response, many unions organized formal strikes, and workers—oil workers, automakers, woodcutters, meatpackers, the list went on—walked off the job. Truman, who knew what it was like to survive on very little money, was sympathetic to the unions. He urged management to grant reasonable pay increases. In early 1946, when the nation's steelworkers threatened to strike if they did not receive a pay increase, Truman worked with their unions to make a proposal to management. When management rejected it, the workers went on strike, and the steel industry came to a standstill. It was a blow to the U.S. economy, as steel was crucial to many industries.

When workers in two other important industries—coal and the railroads—also launched strikes, Truman decided to take drastic steps before the nation's economy collapsed. On the night

Steelworkers picket for better pay outside the Bethlehem Steel Corporation's plant in early 1946.

of May 24, he asked the railroad workers, in particular, to return to work the next day as a matter of duty to their country. When that day came and it looked as though the railroad industry's labor-management squabble was still unresolved, Truman announced that he would draft all striking American workers into the military—where, as their commander-in-chief, he would have the power to order them back to work. The railroad industry soon announced that it had resolved the strike—and it was not long before other strike-paralyzed industries did the same.

Truman impressed fellow politicians as well as millions of ordinary American citizens with his tough stance. He also paid a heavy political price for it—many labor unions that had previously thought of him as a friend were no longer so sure. This change of heart cost Truman many supporters when it came time to run for a second term.

REELECTION

By the spring of 1948, Truman's approval ratings had dipped. Democratic Party leaders were not planning on giving him the presidential nomination for the upcoming election. Instead, they hoped to recruit Dwight D. Eisenhower. Eisenhower, known as Ike, had been one of the heroes of World War II. He had achieved the rank of five-star general and had been supreme commander of Allied forces in Europe and one of the architects of the successful D-Day invasion. He was one of the most popular figures in the country, and the Democrats thought he would make an excellent candidate. In spite of their urgings, however, Eisenhower refused, and the party turned to Truman.

At the Democratic National Convention that July, which was held at Convention Hall in Philadelphia, Truman restated his ongoing commitment to his Fair Deal policies. He then created a stir when he began pushing for improved civil rights for America's minorities. This stand was risky, as it ruffled the feathers not only of the Republican Party but of the Dixiecrats—conservative members of the Democratic Party—as well. This was a time when the notion of treating minorities with equality was still pretty much unthinkable to many Americans.

Harry Truman speaks at the 1948 Democratic National Convention in Philadelphia.

Truman believed in fairness. His goals for minorities included reducing violence against them and giving them full voting rights, and he also wanted to penalize companies that exercised discrimination in their hiring practices. In a speech given before Congress in February 1947, he had said, "The Federal Government has a clear duty to see that the Constitutional guarantees of individual liberties and of equal protection under the laws are not denied or abridged anywhere in the Union. That duty is shared by all three branches of the Government, but it can be filled only if the Congress enacts modern, comprehensive civil rights laws."

During the convention, many Dixiecrats walked out, infuriated over Truman's dedication to civil rights. Their departure made the Democratic Party look divided and weak. Between this tension, the threat of Democratic fatigue sweeping the nation after the long presidential run from Roosevelt to Truman, and the numerous victories scored by the Republican Party in the 1946 midterm elections, Truman's chances of retaining the presidency seemed bleak.

Truman had no intention of giving up without a fight, however. He undertook a 20,000-mile whistle-stop tour across the United States by train to win the hearts and minds of the voters. Instead of reeling from all the criticism hurled at him from both the Republicans and the mutinous Dixiecrats, he went on the offensive and attacked them for refusing to support his programs. He drew large crowds everywhere. In spite of the fact that he was a president running for reelection, he managed to portray himself as the little guy pitted against giants. This endeared him to the average American.

The news media treated Truman like a guaranteed loser and wrote of Thomas E. Dewey—the Republican nominee once again—as if Dewey had already won the election. Dewey, who campaigned very little, seemed to agree. Even polling organizations, whose purpose is to get a sense of the public's feelings and attitudes, stopped taking surveys.

When Election Day arrived on November 2, however, Truman stunned the world by beating Dewey by more than 100 electoral votes—303 to 189. He also received over 2 million

Harry Truman holds up a copy of the Chicago Tribune, *which incorrectly announced Thomas E. Dewey as the winner of the 1948 presidential race.*

more popular votes than Dewey. The following morning, the Chicago *Tribune* suffered considerable embarrassment when the newspaper came out with the headline "Dewey Defeats Truman." Amused by the error, a smiling Truman held up a copy while his picture was taken. It is still one of the most memorable images in American political history.

SECOND TERM AS PRESIDENT

$\mathcal{T}$ruman was inaugurated into his first full term as president on January 20, 1949. Standing in front of the Capitol, he began his inauguration speech around 1:30 p.m. Many expected him to use the opportunity to once again promote his Fair Deal policies. Instead he focused on international matters—specifically the evils of communism. He said, "Communism is based on the belief that man is so weak and inadequate that he is unable to govern himself, and therefore requires the rule of strong masters. Democracy is based on the conviction that man has the moral and intellectual capacity, as well as the inalienable right, to govern himself with reason and fairness." He vowed to continue supporting democratic nations in their fight to resist communist influence and hinted at a new and formal alliance among America and several other nations. He also introduced the idea of making America's scientific and industrial knowledge available to underdeveloped countries.

THE CREATION OF NATO

In March 1948, five nations of western Europe—the United Kingdom, Belgium, the Netherlands, Luxembourg, and France—agreed to an alliance to better protect them against possible hostility by the Soviet Union. This agreement was known as the Treaty of Brussels. It was not long, however, before these nations realized that Soviet military power would still pose a significant threat to

Truman gives his inaugural speech for his second term in office on January 20, 1949.

their security. Discussions then began for a new alliance that would involve other countries, including the United States.

The result of these discussions was the North Atlantic Treaty Organization (NATO). Along with the five Treaty of Brussels nations, NATO included the United States, Canada, Denmark, Italy, Portugal, Norway, and Iceland. The core of the alliance lay in the agreement that an attack on one of the nations would be viewed as an attack on all—and that the other nations would be urged (although not required) to participate in an appropriate response.

NATO was established largely to assure mutual cooperation among nations against any and all military threats. Here, Truman officially enlists the United States in the NATO effort in April 1949.

Truman strongly supported the NATO proposal from the moment it came to him. It was the new alliance he had hinted at during his inaugural speech; he had been involved in negotiating the NATO proposal prior to the election in November. His secretary of state, Dean Acheson, handled many of the details, but Truman drove the process along. He signed the NATO treaty in April, and it was approved by the Senate with little resistance even among Republicans. It is considered by many to be one of the greatest achievements of his presidency. The NATO alliance proved crucial before Truman's second term was over.

The Cold War Heats Up

In spite of Truman's efforts to slow the spread of communism, the Soviets made progress in Europe. In March 1948 they succeeded in overthrowing the Czech government and took control of Czechoslovakia. Around the same time, Truman's approval of U.S. assistance to rebuild areas of Germany that were beyond Soviet control angered Joseph Stalin.

In September 1949, just two months after the U.S. Senate approved the NATO alliance, two events occurred that gave Truman cause for grave concern. First, the forces of a Chinese revolutionary named Mao Zedong defeated the army of China's government (which was supported by the United States); on October 1, Mao proclaimed China a new nation—the People's Republic of China—under communist rule. The immediate formation of an alliance between Stalin and Mao created an even larger communist threat to the United States and its democratic allies. Later that same month, the Soviet

The Berlin Airlift

In response to the U.S. attempt to rebuild areas of Germany beyond Soviet control, Stalin tried to block the flow of crucial supplies to West Berlin. One of Stalin's greatest fears following World War II was a revitalized Germany, a Germany that would be able to defend itself against communist influence. In defiance of Stalin's blockade, the United States, along with several other nations, began flying supplies into West Berlin. This ongoing effort became known as the Berlin Airlift. Stalin eventually removed the blockade in May 1949, but tensions between the Soviet Union and the United States continued to rise.

Union's successful test of an atomic bomb for the third time clearly marked the end of a brief era in which only America possessed this deadly weapon.

Truman was urged by the people in his administration to increase government spending on defense programs in response to this growth of Soviet power and influence. Truman approved the development of a hydrogen bomb (also called a super bomb or H-bomb) that would be more destructive than the atomic bomb.

Truman was also urged to increase spending on the conventional military—planes, tanks, and so on—to get it back up to wartime strength. Although doing so meant taking money away from other programs, in September 1950 he approved a plan to ready the military for full-scale conflict against communist forces. Truman also approved secret efforts to keep communist influence from spreading into governments in Africa, Asia, and Latin America.

Fear of Communism at Home

From the day World War II ended, it seemed, fear of communism began to spread among the people of the United States. First there was the fear that a politically and militarily strong Soviet Union would take over all of Europe and Asia. There were also worries that communists would try to conquer the United States—not with tanks and rifles but by infiltrating the government and influencing high-ranking officials into gradually transitioning the nation into a communistic way of life.

During Truman's first term, the House of Representatives created an investigative committee, the Un-American Activities

Committee, to look into this matter. They pushed Truman to issue an executive order in March 1947 that gave the government the power to question employees whose loyalty was suspect and to remove anyone if it was unconvinced of that loyalty. This same committee amassed evidence that a man named Alger Hiss, a former member of the State Department under both Roosevelt and Truman (during his first term), had been a member of a secret communist network. The thought of such an important official having communist leanings terrified the nation.

When the paranoia reached a fever pitch in early 1950, a Republican senator from Wisconsin named Joseph McCarthy saw an opportunity. McCarthy's first few years in Washington were undistinguished. He was unpopular with the media and with his fellow senators, as he had a prickly, combative personality. Nevertheless he came to national attention after making a series of speeches in which he claimed to have a long list of people working in President Truman's State Department who were known communists. He went on to say that he believed Truman knew of the communist influence and had worked to hide it. He also hinted, although he did not say it outright, that there were communists among Truman's group of closest advisers.

Truman was sympathetic to the fears of the public to some degree. He believed America needed to do everything possible to keep ahead of the Soviet Union in terms of military strength and technology and to continue all efforts to contain communist influence around the world. He had never bought into the notion that communism had taken hold in the American government, however. He knew that there would always be a small degree of infiltration and that it was necessary to weed it out whenever

Senator Joseph McCarthy claimed there was communist infiltration all throughout the American government. But he was a bit too radical in his approach, and his over-the-top tactics eventually got him pushed out of politics for good.

possible. "I am not worried about the Communist Party taking over the government of the United States," he said once, "but I am against a person, whose loyalty is not to the government of the United States, holding a government job." Still, he dismissed the notion that there were communist agents hiding around every corner.

Senator McCarthy, however, had been so successful that Truman felt he had no choice but to respond to McCarthy's accusations. He told the press that McCarthy's charges were unfounded and would not stand up to close examination. He sensed McCarthy and the other Republicans who supported him were simply looking for something they could use against the Democrats in future elections. In response to the claim that his secretary of state, Dean Acheson, had communist ties, Truman said he felt Acheson would, in fact, likely become known as one of the greatest secretaries of state in American history.

In a letter to the sister of a friend who was being personally attacked by McCarthy, Truman wrote, "I think our friend McCarthy will eventually get all that is coming to him." Before long the president was proven correct. McCarthy began to lose the support of both his fellow politicians and the American people. In early December 1954, he was formally condemned for his actions by the Senate, and his reputation quickly declined.

The Korean War

As World War II had drawn to a close, both American and Soviet forces occupied the peninsular nation of Korea. They had originally been there to drive out Japanese forces, but this objective was no longer an issue after Japan surrendered in September 1945. The following December, the United States and the Soviet Union decided to try governing Korea in a kind of political partnership. Divided by a line of latitude located 38 degrees north of the equator—and thereby known as the thirty-eighth parallel—Korea would be ruled by the Soviets in the northern half and America in the southern half. Each side expressed a desire to see Korea return to a single, unified country—but neither was willing to relinquish control of its half in order to make this happen.

On June 24, 1950, North Korean forces crossed the thirty-eighth parallel and invaded South Korea. Their intent, it seemed, was to overthrow the U.S.-sponsored government and take control of the entire country. Although this attack was led by a Korean communist leader named Kim Il Sung, Truman was certain the Soviets were behind it. He was infuriated by their arrogant boldness. Nevertheless he was faced with a grim decision: whether to get America involved in another major conflict just five years after the end of World War II. He was also concerned that any military action in Korea could easily involve and perhaps even spread to other nations—and thus lead to another world war. China, for example, now under communist control, lay to the immediate north and west of Korea. If China got involved—or if the Soviets themselves sent troops—the death toll could quickly reach into the hundreds of thousands.

At the same time, Truman was still committed to the belief that communism was a threat to all free people and therefore could not be allowed to spread under any circumstances. When he received reports that South Korea did not have the military strength to repel the invasion, he knew the success of North Korea was all but certain unless he took action. There was also a sense among Truman's aides that Stalin was testing him to see if he would fight back. If he did not, then perhaps Stalin would try to overthrow other nations as well. In the end, Truman decided that the United States could not stand idly by.

He began by ordering air and sea support for South Korean forces; he did not want to put soldiers on the ground right away. However, when General Douglas MacArthur informed him that it would be impossible to fight off the communists without ground

U.S. troops were sent overseas in 1950 to help the Asian nation of South Korea in its fight against communist forces from neighboring North Korea.

Dismissing a Hero

General Douglas MacArthur (below) criticized Truman publicly for refusing to support his idea of invading the Chinese mainland. As a result, Truman made the controversial decision to relieve MacArthur of his command. MacArthur had been known to show a certain degree of insubordination toward his superiors throughout his military career.

Nevertheless he was very popular among the American people, and Truman's approval rating plummeted. Truman knew his popularity might suffer, but he felt MacArthur's disrespect for the presidency could not be tolerated. He replaced MacArthur with General Matthew Ridgway (right), a brilliant leader who was known—in a very Truman-like way—for addressing the truth of every matter regardless of how he would

be perceived for it. Ridgway quickly solidified American and UN positions along the thirty—eighth parallel and throughout South Korea.
MacArthur, meanwhile, returned to the United States and was given a
hero's welcome that included, among other events, a ticker-tape parade
through the streets of New York City.

support as well, Truman ordered several thousand U.S. soldiers stationed in Japan to move into South Korea immediately.

Truman also knew he needed military assistance from other countries. For this, he turned to the United Nations (UN), an organization formed in 1945 in the interests of peace, economic cooperation, and open dialogue among world governments. UN members swiftly approved a resolution to support U.S. efforts in Korea, and troops from more than a dozen nations eventually became involved. General MacArthur was appointed the military leader of those forces.

Early on, American and UN troops scored significant victories in Korea. MacArthur launched an attack in mid–September that drove communist forces out of the southern areas. Encouraged by this success, Truman authorized MacArthur to continue into North Korea with the ultimate goal of rejoining the North and the South into one nation. In late October, however, China sent troops into the North and drove MacArthur's armies back to the thirty-eighth parallel. When MacArthur suggested broadening the war by committing troops to an assault on China itself, Truman rejected the idea.

The Korean War continued throughout the remainder of Truman's second term as president and beyond, with neither side gaining a clear edge. The conflict ultimately ended in a cease-fire—essentially a stalemate—on July 27, 1953, several months after Truman left office.

One More Strike

In November 1951, as had happened during his first administration, labor-management conflict arose that had the potential to cause the nation great harm. The industry in question was steel manufacturing; with the Korean War in full swing, steel was needed in almost every facet of the military. Without it, America's forces overseas would not be able to sustain the fight for long.

Because of the war, companies were producing steel at record levels, and profits were high. The labor unions, angered that they had not been given significant pay raises, threatened to strike at the end of December. Truman stepped in and asked for a postponement of the strike until the following April in the hope that something could be worked out, and labor agreed. During that period, both sides—labor and management—tried to negotiate a satisfactory arrangement. In response to labor's request for pay hikes, management wanted to increase the price of steel.

With the April deadline approaching, Truman saw that there was no deal in sight. With the threat of a halt in steel production imminent—a halt that might put the lives of American soldiers in danger—Truman acted. On April 8, believing he had no other choice, he ordered that the government take control of all American steel mills.

As a result of his decision, the mills continued to run as before. However, many questioned whether Truman had stepped beyond the boundaries of his presidential power. Thus began a legal battle that ended up in the U.S. Supreme Court. In early June, in a vote of six to three, it was determined that Truman's seizure of the steel industry was, in fact, illegal. After this judicial decision was handed down, the labor unions ordered an immediate strike, and the steel industry came to a halt.

As the strike continued for fifty-three days, millions of tons of steel that were due to be produced were not—and the amount that the military needed dropped by one-third. The laborers who participated in the strike because they wanted more money were now without regular paychecks. At the end of July, Truman called together the leaders of both management and the unions and insisted that they reach an agreement. When they finally did, labor received a modest increase, and the steel industry raised its prices. It was one of the costliest strikes in American history, as well as a historic event in terms of the limits of presidential power.

THE ELECTION OF 1952

Truman was expected to run for another presidential term in the election of 1952. Although the Twenty-second Amendment to the Constitution, which had been ratified in February 1951, limited a president to no more than two full terms of his own, its wording specifically exempted the incumbent president—that is, Truman—from its effect.

In spite of the optimism of the people around him, Truman decided not to run again for a number of reasons. He was tired of the job. He had become frustrated with Congress—under both Republican and Democratic majorities—when it continually refused to support many of his Fair Deal proposals. The war in Korea had also worn him down; it lingered throughout his second term with little hope of a conclusion. In addition, the war was becoming unpopular at home, and as a result, Truman's approval rating with the American people had dropped.

Truman also knew that the reelection campaign would be long and difficult. He thought of his family. His wife. Bess, never liked being first lady, and she held no love for Washington, D.C., and the political scene. She and Margaret had been spending a great deal of time back in Independence, and Truman missed them both very much.

On March 29, during an otherwise unremarkable dinner speech, he said casually to his audience, "I shall not be a

Harry Truman lent his support to presidential candidate Adlai Stevenson during the 1952 elections.

candidate for re-election. I have served my country long, and I think efficiently and honestly. I shall not accept a renomination. I do not feel that it is my duty to spend another four years in the White House."

Truman lent his support to Adlai Stevenson, the governor of Illinois, in the presidential election. Stevenson was articulate, intelligent, and a loyal supporter of Democratic programs. The Republicans chose Dwight D. Eisenhower. Truman, in fact, had urged Eisenhower, whom he had known for years, to run as the Democratic candidate before getting behind Stevenson, but Eisenhower gave in to his Republican leanings. When Truman heard of his decision to run as a Republican, his reply gave some insight into his own opinion of the presidency: "I'm sorry to see these fellows get Ike into this business. They're showing him gates of gold and silver, which will turn out [to be] copper and tin."

Eisenhower won the presidency in November. Meanwhile, the sixty-eight-year-old Truman began thinking about what he wanted to do with the rest of his life.

LATER YEARS

Truman never had any doubts about where he would go once his presidency was over. Eisenhower was sworn in as his successor on January 20, 1953, and Truman and his wife got on a train headed for Independence the same day. Thousands stood along the tracks and greeted them along the way. When they arrived in Independence that night, they were unprepared for the cheering crowd of about 10,000 that awaited them. Truman was deeply touched by this outward show of appreciation.

TRUMAN AS PRIVATE CITIZEN

Truman settled back into ordinary life as quickly as possible. He and Bess moved into his old family home, which he had inherited. This house suited him. He had not been wealthy when he became president, and he was not returning to Independence a wealthy man. He was content to live in an ordinary house on an ordinary street.

Because he now seemed like every other average person, people often felt they were welcome to come by and knock on his door whenever they wished. Truman was patient and understanding with these visitors, but every now and then there was a problem. His daughter, Margaret, later remembered one such incident: "There was a man who walked up to the front gate and insisted he had to see the President. One look and it was clear to us that he was a nut. We called the police, and they responded promptly. At the station house they discovered that he had recently been discharged from a mental institution in

Crowds form in front of the Truman home in Independence, Missouri, upon the return of the president and the First Lady.

Pennsylvania. He had written Dad several threatening letters and had a loaded .45 revolver in his pocket."

In the immediate future, Truman simply wanted to relax and enjoy life. He and Bess did some traveling; they spent a month in Hawaii and later traveled by car back to Washington (they did the driving themselves). In May 1956 they toured Europe for two months. Truman was treated like a celebrity everywhere he went.

In April 1956 Margaret got married, and she had the first of four sons in June 1957.

Memoirs

Truman wanted to earn an income in his post-presidency years. He was offered executive positions in a number of businesses and was invited to make product endorsements and to engage in

Writers Are Born, Not Made

Truman was to regret agreeing to produce his memoirs in one significant way—he had had no idea how difficult it could be to write a book. A small staff was hired to help out with a variety of tasks, among them the organization of literally thousands of papers from his time in office and checking the accuracy of all the facts that ended up in the manuscript. Truman did some of the writing himself, but other parts were the product of ghostwriters, who then went over every line of their work with Truman for his approval or adjustment; this stage was a normal part of the writing and editing process. There were times when his assistants had to speak with old political friends instead of going to Truman directly because the former president found it too frustrating.

political lobbying and consulting work of various sorts. However, he wanted projects that he considered more legitimate.

About a month after he returned to Independence, he was asked by the publisher of *Life* magazine to write a book about his presidential experiences. Truman was attracted to the idea of being able to tell his side of the story, to set down the historical record. He was also no doubt pleased by the fact that the publisher had offered him more than a half-million dollars for the manuscript—money that would enable him and Bess to live very comfortably for the rest of their lives.

The finished book was supposed to be about 300,000 words long, but by the spring of 1955, it had grown to nearly 2 million and needed to be cut down. In the end, *Life* magazine published the memoirs in segments, over multiple issues, and another publishing company, Doubleday, released the hardcover book. Because of its length, Doubleday published it in two volumes. The first volume, *Memoirs: Year of Decisions*, came out in November 1955. The second, *Years of Trial and Hope, 1946–1952*, was released in spring 1956. They sold well and were generally liked by both the critics and the general public. They also served to improve Truman's reputation by stressing how difficult his presidency had been.

THE TRUMAN LIBRARY

One of Truman's most cherished projects after returning to Independence was overseeing the construction of his presidential library. He originally wished for it to be built on the family farm in Grandview; his brother, Vivian, had even picked out a site. That decision was changed, however, when the town of Independence donated thirteen acres of land not far from Truman's home. Truman made some rough drawings of how he hoped the library would look; he sketched a building similar to his grandfather's house, which had been demolished in his childhood.

Truman decided that none of the money for the construction of the library would come from the government. Instead he participated in numerous fund-raising activities in the hope of gathering enough money on his own. In the end, he received nearly a million dollars for the project; he had thoroughly enjoyed the work he put into giving speeches, shaking hands, and writing letters to solicit money. All told, he received more than 17,000 donations.

The library was completed in July 1957. The final design was not anything like the drawings Truman had made of his grandfather's home. From a bird's-eye point of view, it has a crescent shape. It is only one story but has a large basement. It contained more than three million papers from Truman's private collection at the start, and many more came in the years ahead. At the dedication ceremony, Truman welcomed a long line of old friends, including several senators, members of his administration, the former first lady Eleanor Roosevelt, and the former president Herbert Hoover, as well as family members, neighbors,and thousands of other Independence residents.

Another of the distinguished guests, Chief Justice of the Supreme Court Earl Warren, gave a speech at the ceremony in

Herbert Hoover (center left) and Harry Truman (center right) at the dedication ceremony of the Truman Library in Independence, Missouri.

Truman in his later years. By the mid-1960s his health had begun to seriously decline.

which he stated, "I dedicate this building as a museum and a library to safeguard, exhibit, and facilitate the use of its valuable resources that the American people, and all the peoples of this earth, may gain by their wide and wise use understanding of ourselves and our times, and wisdom to choose the right paths in the years that lie ahead." The library was one of Truman's proudest achievements following his presidency, and he spent much of his retirement time in his private office there.

Illness and Death

Truman had always been known for his good health. Even into his seventies, he seemed fit and energetic. Although in June 1954 he had an emergency operation to remove his appendix and gallbladder, he soon recovered and was back to his usual busy pace. His health began to decline in the early 1960s. He was not moving at the same spry pace as before, and his hearing began to fade. In the fall of 1964, he fell in his home and cracked two ribs. He was never the same afterward. He became thin, pale, and fragile. As he struggled with a number of other health issues in the years ahead, he was seen less and less in public. In December 1972, he was admitted to the local hospital with problems in his lungs, heart, and kidneys. Truman slipped into a coma on Christmas Day, and he died less than twenty-four hours later, on December 26. He was eighty-eight years old.

Legacy

Harry S. Truman came into the presidency during one of the most turbulent periods in American history. He oversaw the completion of World War II and less than a decade later committed the nation to another war, in Korea. Throughout his time in office, the United States and the Soviet Union were involved in a cold war. Some considered it little more than a conflict of ideas, but in Truman's eyes, it was a struggle between the forces of good and evil. Although he left office with one of the lowest approval ratings of any president, with the passage of time, his reputation grew. His dedication to decency, honesty, and old-fashioned common sense eventually endeared him in the public's mind. As his daughter later wrote in a biography of her father toward the end of his life, "He is, of course, pleased when he hears that one historian or another, or a group of historians, has rated him as one of the eight or nine greatest Presidents in our history."

The presidency of Harry Truman took place during a tumultuous time in U.S. history. The legacy he left was that of a man who handled tremendous challenges with honesty and integrity. Historians have since ranked him among the nation's greatest leaders.

TIMELINE

1884
Born in Lamar, Missouri, on May 8

1901
Graduates from high school

1917
Joins the military to participate in World War I

1919
Marries Elizabeth "Bess" Wallace

1922
Wins first political election and becomes Jackson County judge

1934
Wins election to the U.S. Senate

1880

1940
Wins reelection to the U.S.
Senate

1944
Becomes vice president of the
United States

1945
Becomes president of the
United States upon the death
of Franklin D. Roosevelt

1948
Is elected president in his
own right

1972
Dies at the age of eighty-
eight

1980

NOTES

CHAPTER ONE

p.10, "Vivian and I used to play in the south pasture . . .": Robert H. Ferrell, *The Autobiography of Harry S. Truman* (Columbia: University of Missouri Press, 2002), p. 6.

p.11, ". . . loved to sing when the family spent time around the piano . . .": Robert H. Ferrell, *Harry S. Truman: A Life* (Columbia: University of Missouri Press, 1995), p. 5.

p.16, "The hall there could hold . . . ": Merle Miller, *Plain Speaking: An Oral Biography of Harry S. Truman* (New York: Berkley, 1974), p. 117.

CHAPTER TWO

p.20, "Nobody was ever good enough for her, or so it seemed . . .": Janey Chiles, in Miller, *Plain Speaking*, p. 104.

p.21, "Once committed to . . .": John Keegan, *The First World War* (New York: Knopf, 1999), p. 373.

p.23, "Although they were standing at attention . . .": David McCullough, *Truman* (New York: Simon and Schuster, 1992), p. 117.

p.24, "He came out of the army convinced . . .": Margaret Truman, *Harry S. Truman* (New York: William Morrow and Company, 1973), p. 60.

p.26, "Even before my father came back from France . . .": Truman, *Harry S. Truman*, p. 61.

CHAPTER THREE

p.32, "I'm kind to people . . .": Tom Pendergast, in Lawrence H. Larsen and Nancy J. Hulston, *Pendergast!* (Columbia: University of Missouri Press, 1997), p. 71.

p.32, "They were fundamentally opposites. Truman was a country man . . .": Robert H. Ferrell, *Truman and Pendergast* (Columbia: University of Missouri Press, 1999), p. 4.

p.34, "The record of the county court is refreshing . . .": McCullough, *Truman*, p. 170.

p.34, "To even talk about throwing [Truman] out of office . . .": McCullough, *Truman*, p. 170.

p.35, "The county was in debt when I got in . . .": Harry Truman, in Miller, *Plain Speaking*, p. 130.

CHAPTER FOUR

p.39, ". . . was coming to the end of his second, and by custom last . . .": Ferrell, *Harry S. Truman*, p. 128.

p.40, "Word hard, keep your mouth shut . . .": Tom Pendergast, in McCullough, *Truman*, p. 213.

p.42, "In the Senate he was . . . ignored . . .": Ferrell, *Harry S. Truman*, p. 133.

★ ★ ★ ★ ★ ★ ★ ★ ★ ★ ★ ★ ★ ★ ★ ★ ★ ★ ★

p.55, "Is there anything *we* can do for *you*?": Harry S. Truman, *Memoirs*, vol. 1, *Year of Decisions* (Garden City, NY: Doubleday, 1955), p. 5.

p.55, "Boys if you ever pray, pray for me now . . .": McCullough, *Truman*, p. 353.

CHAPTER FIVE

p.56, "The situation for Germany was quite hopeless . . .": Alan Axelrod, *The Real History of World War II: A New Look at the Past* (New York: Sterling, 2008), p. 327.

p.56, "For the Japanese warrior, the only honorable alternative . . .": Axelrod, *The Real History of World War II*, p. 334.

p.59, "In 1945 I had the A Bomb dropped on Japan . . .": Robert H. Ferrell, ed., *Off the Record: The Private Papers of Harry S. Truman* (New York: Harper and Row, 1980), p. 304.

p.64, "This twenty-one-point message . . .": Truman, *Memoirs*, vol. 1, p. 481.

p.68, "The Federal Government has a clear duty to see . . .": McCullough, *Truman*, p. 587.

CHAPTER SIX

p.71, "Communism is based on the belief that man is so weak and inadequate . . .": McCullough, *Truman*, p. 730.

p.78, "I am not worried about the Communist Party taking over the government . . .": McCullough, *Truman*, p. 552.

p.79, "I think our friend McCarthy will eventually get . . .": Harry Truman, in Robert J. Donovan, *Tumultuous Years: The Presidency of Harry S. Truman, 1949–1953* (Columbia: University of Missouri Press, 1996), p. 170.

p.87, "I shall not be a candidate for re-election . . .": Harry S. Truman, *Memoirs*, vol. 2, *Years of Trial and Hope, 1946–1952* (Garden City, NY: Doubleday, 1955), p. 492.

p.88, "I'm sorry to see these fellows get Ike into this business . . .": Harry Truman, in Donovan, *Tumultuous Years*, p. 394.

CHAPTER SEVEN

p.89, "There was a man who walked up to the front gate . . .": Truman, *Harry S. Truman*, p. 561.

p.95, "I dedicate this building as a museum and a library . . .": McCullough, *Truman*, p. 961.

p.96, "He is, of course, pleased when he hears . . .": Truman, *Harry S. Truman*, p. 580.

★ ★ ★ ★ ★ ★ ★ ★ ★ ★ ★ ★ ★ ★ ★ ★ ★ ★ ★ ★

GLOSSARY

Allies a group of nations that formed the eventual victorious side of World War I. A similar group used the same name during World War II.

Central Powers a group of nations that formed the eventual losing side of World War I

communist someone who believes that people should put their individual rights and freedoms second to the "greater good" of their community

conservative in politics, someone who believes in the philosophy of a smaller government, lower taxes (and thus fewer government programs), and adherence to traditions

consortium in business, a group of people who have joined together to achieve a set of common goals

creditor someone who lends money or goods with the agreement that they will be paid for at a later date

democratic referring to the form of government in which ultimate authority is considered to reside in those who are governed

Democratic National Convention the meeting of all leading members of the Democratic Party, usually to nominate candidates for future elections and to discuss and debate the party's forthcoming policies

economic concerning the financial system of a government and its people

electoral vote a vote cast through the electoral college system

Freemasons a largely secret organization that emphasizes cooperation among its members, as well as a desire to do charitable works for the world at large

incumbent the current holder of a position or an office, especially a political one

inflation the disproportionate rising of prices in relation to the income of citizens

liberal in politics, a philosophy of larger government, higher taxes to fund government programs, and the belief that change and innovation usually lead to progress

Medicare a government program of health care, especially for citizens over the age of sixty-five

political machine a largely unseen, often secretive, group of people who control the actions and policies of a political party

regulation the government practice of controlling the businesses of a nation, usually for the purpose of protecting consumers

segregationist a person who favors the social separation, usually enforced, of groups or classes of people, generally by race or religion

speculator in business, one who takes risks (usually with the investment of money) with hope of large rewards

theater in terms of warfare, a large geographic area in which many battles and sustained campaigns are fought

FURTHER INFORMATION

BOOKS

Burgan, Michael. *Hiroshima: Birth of the Nuclear Age*. Tarrytown, NY: Marshall Cavendish Benchmark, 2010.

Elish, Dan. *Franklin Delano Roosevelt*. Tarrytown, NY: Marshall Cavendish Benchmark, 2008.

Fitzgerald, Brian. *The Korean War: America's Forgotten War*. Mankato, MN: Compass Point Books, 2006.

Isserman, Maurice. *World War II*. New York: Chelsea House, 2010.

World War II. Tarrytown, NY: Marshall Cavendish Benchmark, 2011.

DVDs

American Experience: Truman. PBS Home Video. 2006.

Korea, The Forgotten War. A&E Home Video. 2005.

Truman. SoundWorks. 2006.

WEBSITES

American Experience: Truman

www.pbs.org/wgbh/amex/truman/

Based on the Truman documentary from the *American Experience* series. Includes biographical information, a detailed timeline, a media gallery, and educational resources.

Harry S. Truman Biography

www.biography.com/articles/Harry-S.-Truman-9511121

Brief but solid biography. Also includes links to other people prominent in Truman's life.

Harry S. Truman Library and Museum

www.trumanlibrary.org/

Home page of the Harry S. Truman Library and Museum. The plentiful resource information includes online documents, historic photographs, and podcasts.

BIBLIOGRAPHY

BOOKS

Ambrose, Stephen E. *D-Day—June 6, 1944: The Climactic Battle of World War II*. New York: Touchstone Books, 1994.

———. *Eisenhower, Soldier and President*. New York: Touchstone Books, 1990.

Axelrod, Alan. *The Real History of World War II: A New Look at the Past*. New York: Sterling, 2008.

Dallek, Robert. *Harry S. Truman*. New York: Times Books, 2008.

Dollinger, Hans. *The Decline and Fall of Nazi Germany and Imperial Japan: A Pictorial History of the Final Days of World War II*. New York: Bonanza Books, 1965.

Donovan, Robert J. *Conflict and Crisis: The Presidency of Harry S. Truman, 1945–1948*. Columbia: University of Missouri Press, 1996.

———. *Tumultuous Years: The Presidency of Harry S. Truman, 1949–1953*. Columbia: University of Missouri Press, 1996.

Ferguson, Niall. *The Pity of War: Explaining World War I*. New York: Basic Books, 1999.

Ferrell, Robert H. *Harry S. Truman: A Life*. Columbia: University of Missouri Press, 1995.

———. *Truman and Pendergast*. Columbia: University of Missouri Press, 1999.

———, ed. *Off the Record: The Private Papers of Harry S. Truman*. New York: Harper and Row, 1980.

Giangreco, D. M. *The Soldier from Independence: A Military Biography of Harry Truman*. Osceola, WA: Zenith Press, 2009.

Gilbert, Martin. *The Second World War: A Complete History*. New York: Henry Holt, 2004.

Kaufman, Burton I. *The Korean Conflict*. Westport, CT: Greenwood Press, 1999.

Keegan, John. *The First World War*. New York: Knopf, 1999.

Keyes, Ralph. *The Wit and Wisdom of Harry Truman: A Treasury of Quotations, Anecdotes, and Observations*. New York: HarperCollins, 1995.

Larsen, Lawrence H., and Nancy J. Hulston, *Pendergast!* Columbia: University of Missouri Press, 1997.

McCullough, David. *Truman*. New York: Simon and Schuster, 1992.

Miller, Merle. *Plain Speaking: An Oral Biography of Harry S. Truman*. New York: Berkley, 1974.

Schrecker, Ellen. *The Age of McCarthyism: A Brief History with Documents*. New York: Bedford Books, 1994.

Stueck, William. *The Korean War: An International History*. Princeton, NJ: Princeton University Press, 1995.

Truman, Harry S. *Memoirs*. Vol. 1, *Year of Decisions*. Garden City, NY: Doubleday, 1955.

———. *Memoirs*. Vol. 2, *Years of Trial and Hope, 1946–1952*. Garden City, NY: Doubleday, 1955.

Truman, Margaret. *Harry S. Truman*. New York: William Morrow, 1973.

INDEX

INDEX

★ ★ ★ ★ ★ ★ ★ ★ ★ ★ ★ ★ ★ ★ ★ ★ ★ ★

★ ★ ★ ★ ★ ★ ★ ★ ★ ★ ★ ★ ★ ★ ★ ★ ★

ABOUT THE AUTHOR

Wil Mara is the award-winning author of more than 120 books. He has written both fiction and nonfiction, for children and adults, including several other titles in Marshall Cavendish's Presidents and Their Times series. More information about his work can be found at www.wilmara.com.